Backlit

Liz Robbins

Rattle | Studio City, California | 2025

Backlit
Copyright © 2025 by Liz Robbins

All rights reserved

Layout and design by Timothy Green

Cover art by Sara Pedigo
"Haley's Court," (2025) Acrylic on Paper, 9" x 6"

ISBN: 978-1-931307-63-5

First edition

Rattle Foundation
12411 Ventura Blvd
Studio City, CA 91604
www.rattle.com

The Rattle Foundation is an independent 501(c)3 nonprofit, whose mission is to promote the practice of poetry, and which is not affiliated with any other organization. All poems are works of the imagination. While the perceptions and insights are based on the author's interviews, all names and likenesses to actual individuals have been changed, and no reference to any real person is intended or should be inferred.

Contents

This Game Is a Rip	9
Dilemmas	10
War	12
A Little TV	14
The Desperate Attract the Using	16
Smell of Pitch	18
Sex Worker	19
Small Towns	20
Sex Worker	22
Runaways	23
Sex Worker	24
Dirty Talk	25
Mug Shot	27
Family	28
Once in a Foreign City, I Saw a Dead Body	29
Cigarettes	30
Crying for Money	31
Element of Conflict	32
Desert Scene	33
Sex Worker	34
Daphne, Swimming	35
Manifesto	36
Hiker	37
Clean	39

Acknowledgments	41

Backlit

for the powerless

This Game Is a Rip

The city I come from was split into parts
by a river, its tributaries. Everyone knew

goodness, gauged how deep its well
in everyone else. A black dog, Rover,

stalked the night streets, lining the minds
of housebound women. Watery circles

on tables where glasses of gin had been.
The heart, stopped at the start of an engine.

At sixteen, I owned nothing. Fear, gone,
stuck back in the heads of mothers.

I confessed, gave myself away at makeshift
fires in the woods. So many fallen dead trees.

If I owned things, I didn't know it or love
them enough. Instead, I developed habits.

Cranked heavy metal, inhaled and coughed.
Anything to step deep into the boats

of boys, the boats of their fathers, anything
to flee, though the river whirled endless,

dark. My face burned by the sun, all the tiny
whispers. My town, where boys gauged me.

Then the girls. Now I wake to what sounds
like a shot, like a coin dropping into a slot.

Dilemmas

The john says, I don't care, you decide
        the position this time—and I think about my divorced

stepdad, just before I split at seventeen.
        He'd say, I don't care what we have for dinner, you

decide, you're making it, and I'd be stumped.
        How necessary it seemed to please. I'd hint for clues:

How do you feel about meatloaf? We have meat
        in the fridge ... Anything, anything, he'd say. He really

didn't care in the way some women do, food
        to show love, food to soothe hurts. To him, food was fuel.

Chicken would do, so would hot dogs. Dog
        biscuits, in a pinch. But still it felt like a quiz I might fail,

and I'd make salad, he'd take a few bites,
        declare himself not hungry. An hour later, wolfing down

cereal, surfing porn. Then many beers. Then
        lurching into my room. But this was proof, wasn't it, that

he loved me? That he let me choose? Still I
        try to read what men want without their having to say, so

I won't be hurt or left. I want to tell the john,
        I don't want sex, it's your fantasy I'm loving this. But then

I'd have told the truth, pierced the veil. The john
    would droop. Pimp Mike would be mad. Mike says we girls

are lucky to choose—how many men
    a day, five to ten. But we all know his favorite girls are tens.

War

Jade tells me to think of it as an art.
        When the john walks in and starts unbuckling, to not feel

the scampering heart, the hitch in the belly,
        but to craft a mind like night-blooming jasmine tumbling

down a stone wall. She says, Tell yourself,
        this is my dance. I think of the collage I saw just before I

dropped out of school, Picasso's *Guernica*—
        the mother with her dead baby in her hands, victims of a

bombing, the mother's head thrown
        back, wailing to the sky. The wild-eyed horse grimacing,

rearing back in revolt. My teacher said
        the point of art is to unsettle, but the artist controls what he

makes, and when the john is inside me,
        thrusting roughly, I am less the artist, more the mother crying

out. I take money to lie, to sit astride,
        to ride again the horse from which I'm thrown. Jade says no:

since the beginning, artists have made
        art to change public perception, but that's not their main drive.

They make to escape what's real, to dive
        into their own minds and forget. You can lose yourself, too,

she says, if you try. Jade has hair she's dyed
        black and straightened, round eyes. I listen to her and absorb

what she's saying as if I'm not in the habit
 of making up my own mind. One day, I'll save enough cash

to have my own studio and a vase with a long-
 stemmed rose and thorns. My place will be so quiet, I'll hear

the faraway gallop of a horse as it flees across
 the valley, the whish of a brush on canvas, the cry of a baby.

A Little TV

sits by my bed	about to die	hanging on	I steal cable
from next door	Pimp Mike knows	how to splice	Before The Life
I believed	how they show	call girls	on TV:
the red	gowns, wine	big	operas,
or street-girls	in shorts	hopped up	on meth
I spend more	minutes on	beds w/men	than you'd
imagine	it's not as bad	as you think	the plain
work boots	rough knuckles	simple mealy	smell of worn
underpants	it's worse	than you think	the time
between	when I'm left	with thoughts	gone the wild
blank field	dug out	a bit more	by each trick
I blot	the graphics	w/TV	fill the minutes
w/shows		I am the show	
I'm watching	zoned out	in heels	white undies
sliding open	a drawer	there's a man	speaking
w/twenties	condoms	lube	a little blow

14

this is what	I do	I watch	I connect and
I can't turn down	the sound I can't	shut off	the show

The Desperate Attract the Using

> *The prostitute is a scapegoat; man vents*
> *his turpitude upon her, and he rejects her.*
> —Simone de Beauvoir

The johns come to me, desperate
for fun, a bit frantic with the naughty
thrill of breaking the law and maybe
my spirit. In disguise, in a black dress
and lipstick, thong underwear I'd never
wear alone, I open my body, driven
toward money, desperate to survive,
like any wild animal. The johns read me
as eager for love, as that's the advertising,
the song I sing they pay for. I play
scapegoat for the johns, for the whole
city. Haunted families pick the weak
to carry shame. The friends I keep
are few. I live downtown, far inside
the brick walls, far outside the garden
communities. When I sit beside
the laundromat's purring machines,
I prop up a book I don't read, so
I don't have to engage. All exchanges
lead to, So what do you do? Faces open
with curiosity, tinged with disgust.
I'm too eager for closeness, desperation
cinched to my frame like a trench coat.
A human problem is too much wanting.
We're wired for discontent, for how else
do we progress? Someday, I'll become
a librarian, keeping myself hidden, finding
a place within stacks of books. Knowledge
like scripture. Libraries offering sanctuary

like the churches of old. My footfalls
in the stone aisles like anyone's, like
everyone's: echoing for a brief time,
then gone.

Smell of Pitch

I always go a little further than allowed. I started
tricking at fourteen because my mom needed more
money and my sisters were still young. Too familiar,
the hot asphalt down the street from our driveway,
the lamppost I'd lean against to smoke: the exhaust
from trucks once loaded with lumber and bricks, now
cruising, drivers with popped-top beers. Always, my
feet jammed into white high heels, my legs sore from
standing. The men were nicer then, when I was young.
I had lots of johns. I wore a little black skirt and lace top,
a tiny gold cross. Lots of minutes—whole blocks—
of nothing but distant sound: a building's A/C, a siren,
a kid's scream. I'd space out and think about places
I'd been to as a little kid. Once, my dad came to get me
for my birthday, drove us to a forest two hours away.
I didn't really know him, but early messages make
an impression. We rumbled down a dirt road not saying
a word, little spurts of fear. Then came a fork in the road
with signs: to the right Hikers and to the left No
Admittance. We turned to the left. A mile in, he parked,
and we got out, the pine trees silent. If I'd heard a limb
snap, I'd have pictured bears or bad men. I heard nothing.
We walked in silence an hour, and I looked at dirt, needles,
mushrooms, inhaled the damp. I've never felt closer to
death, more at peace. He picked me a bunch of leaves, then
brought me home. Back on the street, still as a pine, I stand
and wait for a truck to roll to a stop. Someday, I'll build a
cabin in the forest, and I'll hear and feel and fear nothing.

Sex Worker

Out the apartment window I smoke, watch
the sun bake the trees. In my thin blue tank,

I can smell myself. I stub out the filter, light
another. Before the next trick, I might read

or watch TV, but there I'd find dreams, plans,
women my age wearing suits like powerful

men. Better to keep things to the pane, the sky,
the trees. Just basic living. Turning my back

toward the bed, I pop my third downer. In time,
the stillness in the trees will turn to snow. Then

the blizzard inside turns, becomes no danger.

Small Towns

run on it like gasoline. You can smell it
hanging in the First Baptist, the United
Methodist, the Circle K, the Jiffy Lube.
Fear. Gone for a second as I bite into
a gas-station hot dog, scratch off the ticket,
tune out a sermon about where we're
headed. Gone on a Friday night as I head
to the high school, cheer the quarterback
as helmets crack, beer mugs toast, short-
skirted girls back-flip to hip-hop. On
Sundays, I glide out beyond the oak
doors of the church, scan signs propped
in yards: a dictator running for something,
from something, running to run things.
Fear makes me want to hand him the
reign, ha. Tonight I'll pull on lace
stockings, pin them to the garters all
the johns love. I'll open my laptop and
test the mic, zoom the lens. All us girls
now our own pimps, all gone online.
Lured by fear, power, or the evolution
of good tech, solid hard drives. And
who among us doesn't love privacy?
Tomorrow, I'll cover up my heart in
a dress strewn with poppies. Attend
the service at First Baptist because
I'm nothing if not superstitious, and
the songs remind me inside I'm pure
child. Small towns dotted with signs:
Jesus Loves You, Mister for President,
signs telling me what I really want is

my dead father back, telling me how
to be. But what can I do to avoid a hard
life? It is a hard life. In big cities, too.

Sex Worker

One year in The Life
and Pimp Mike takes a few
of us girls to the beach to
celebrate. We don't have
suits, so we wear our bras
and panties. I keep looking
for signs. The gull on the
boardwalk looks straight
at me, turns away. The sand
goes silent a million miles,
out to the Atlantic that goes
a million more. We trudge
over dunes stuck with long,
dry grass. Mike just picks
a spot, tells us to sit. Froth
caps the waves. I wade in,
looking for signs. The waves
roll over, break, withdraw.
The sun slides back behind
a cloud. When I get out, you
can see through. Mike wants
it for free. The girls hop up
for a walk down the beach,
not looking back, not wanting
to check. I want to laugh
hysterically, go to sleep. I kneel,
bend my head, wait for signs.
Nowhere do we have cream,
a radio, chips. I could get
burned. I could grow lost or
hungry. Late tonight, I'll
think of Mike's hand,
gentle on my neck.

Runaways

The impulse to break. When I ran away at fourteen, I didn't know
I was listening to an animal urge to find my own way, like all
teens. When I'm alone, I close my eyes to hear the trailer trucks

thrum by on the highway, one or two braking outside my motel.
I concentrate on their sounds so I can sleep, so I can get through
a man. I've tried to know what these married men want, their

lust to break like mine in reverse. They have a family, but want
something all their own. Maybe I remind them of a high school
crush they never got. A cheerleader, cartwheeling across a wet

field at night. A nurse bending over, sewing up a wound. All our
lives, we are left by people, and our work is to keep finding more.
I have friends. Cara sits with her long brown hair and nose ring,

steaming coffee in her mug, her mouth blowing cigarette smoke.
We complain about the johns, and in our likenesses, feel love for
each other, feel understood. If she's had it worse one night, black

eye or bruises on her wrists where he held her down, I feel sad and
under that, lucky. I've had my share. And always I wonder when
Cara will leave me. Who will come next? There is no one

right way to walk through this life. Yet no one told me at fourteen
what I was really choosing to hold close was the squeal of brakes,
a sound of resistance, like hinges when a door slams shut.

Sex Worker

I.

Margaret Atwood wrote men are afraid
women will laugh at them, women are afraid men will
kill them.

I'm not sure yet if men are afraid. I feel terror's thrill
as I roll up a stocking. How such a small hole can
rip into ruin.

Not all of them burrowed animals emerging into night,
dark into dark, eager to consume,
destroy.

II.

Workman's boots mean his money's hard won.
Like mine. Hands built to manipulate

a slipped wire or smoking hood or sharpened ax.
The head needing to be both

focused and totally gone. The job more dangerous
than fishing Alaska's icy seas

or felling redwoods. I get attacked once a month.
But going to the cops means I've turned

myself in. Instead, in red nails and heels, I turn
myself out—

Dirty Talk

Always cock, which implies
                        a saucy attitude.
Or dick, meaning   jerk.

Always cunt, a mean woman,
                        ugly.
Or pussy, meaning fearful.

Never penis or vagina, clinical
terms suggesting too much
the impersonal.

We want it in your face. We don't
want   polite parlor talk.
We want   low-down.

Penis and vagina reminds us
of when we were unsure,
                        innocent.

We don't want purity. We want
someone   who's taking
responsibility   for what
they choose.

Or no.
We don't want responsible, exactly.

But close. What we want is
a response. What we want is
close.
Down there. Responding.

[...]

You and me, together.
You and me. But not wholly.
Broken.   In parts.
Playing   our parts.

Mug Shot

Because I'd been arrested for arrogance and entitlement—
not to mention stupidity— I met the other misdemeanors
at Hannah Park on Saturdays for community service:
an imperfect punishment, but shot through with the essential
humility, hours in summer sun, riding the back of a trash truck,
hopping off to pick up garbage spreading the trailer camps.
I wore shorts and a bikini, the guys just shorts, and sweat
poured down our necks and bellies as we dreamed aloud
of golden tap beer, counting down the required hours.
The choice to break laws is to assume one's above them, so
to skewer other people's trash with little sticks helped with
perspective. But in truth, it was a bit too carefree, the two bikers
ripping free jokes, poking fun at themselves and everyone, noticing
all, including my chest. The leader looked me in the eye
once with a smile, asked, Quarters or dimes? I loved picturing
his long hair blowing back as he rode, even missed him when I
returned home: still living deep in my mother's casseroles, my
dad's rent-free rooms. At night, gazing out my bedroom window,
I'd recall the stick poking through, pinning for good crumpled
trash, and beyond, wind carrying dead leaves up into bubbly
intoxication, how they seemed to dance freely through the air.

Family

Pimp Mike tells us girls
      again we're like a close family. I think we're more like

a band of secrets that relates by mere proximity, a hostel that takes

care of each other like
      unsolvable problems. We drown out the whispers, the crying,

like a stone wall blocks the sea wind, a wall left with slits and dings

and hollows. With barbs,
      we slice each other's hearts: the Greeks called it sarcasm,

a tearing of the flesh. We say it's to keep us all tough, a boon to our

business, but some of us
      secretly like to give or receive pain, what we learned early.

I'm Angela, the white rock, the bright-hard queen, Pimp Mike's most

righteous hand. I send
      the youngest of us out into the night to find new caves to mine.

Because why not? Why should she be exempt from the work most wet,

most dark, most deep? I've
      done it all my life, exiling Christy—my sister, myself—from

home. And when she comes back that first night, there's no power like

mine, her cash limp in my
      hand, and I imagine I can taste the salt on her thighs, her cheeks.

Once in a Foreign City, I Saw a Dead Body

Riding in a car toward the city
center, I had nothing—
no language, no ties.
But windows.
I looked and looked.
The brown government housing
with its white sheets like flags
waving on lines. The trees like ours,
but smaller, darker.
How tender was I, to view so innocently?
To make such judgments.
To not think through
a scrim of generosity.
The sun and exhaust made bleary
waves of heat. We stopped
in traffic, inched forward
toward an opening.
Then I saw. Too soon
even for an ambulance.
Bald, pale, lying in the street. Gentle
pool of blood by his head. Elderly.
So tender, the skin of his slack mouth,
that I dreamed him a baby,
I dreamed him young and in love.
Then we were gone,
and the small space he opened
stayed open.

Cigarettes

The sex worker gives away
her body: her mouth, her nipples,
her mind. We say, they were giving
it away, about a store with goods
priced unusually low. The street
walker does go low: $15 for a blow,
$25 for sex. She bends down, she
bends over, lies beneath. The john's
car seconds as a motel bed. The dash
lit up like a plane, Johnny Cash
in the background. The best drug
remains anticipation, as the act
itself is never what we dreamed.
After, we're a little let down, emptied.
The sex worker opens the car door,
scans the street for a store to buy
Marlboros, all she wants. He'll drive
home darkly, fresh rationales singing
in his head. All inside, she's a column
of gray, a building on fire, a house
that's leaning, trying and failing to
run from the flames. In her head,
she's trained herself to hear only
the most recent tape: I walk the line.
Over and over, from the top floor,
only smoke escapes.

Crying for Money

I'm not an actress
but an amalgamation
of what the good girl
learns young.
Like philanthropy, tears
etched in shame-dirt
cheeks are something
privileged reason drops
checks on to make
disappear. Which is not
to say adult female
grief shown doesn't
provoke critique,
the delicate pink tulip
petal torn, tearing
itself: the porn
rape scene prompting
one man's slip into
the waistband, another's
spasm with rage.
Crying a hard release
gone liquid as any.
Let go into my hands
your guilt. Since before
Christ, pure girl salt
is mint. Coined.
Mined rocks I work
to make mine.

Element of Conflict

Each night, I walk Phillips Highway in a tiny denim skirt.
    I sway in my high shoes.

Many times an hour, I smoke, sometimes rock in a glass pipe.
    Tell me, do I feel dread

or relief when the unwashed truck cruises to a halt? Is it just me,
    or me against men?

Does sundown ask to find a bed I can use? Wet bills counted
    twice, stuffed in a bag

beside the mace. This car pulling over, that one, glint of a knife,
    edge of a fist. Tell me,

is it just me, or me against nature? As I walk Phillips Highway
    past dusk, under hidden

stars, terror-dreaming of bread and danger in not-so-distant
    rooms, terror-dreaming

as if in prayer, trapped in delusion's cuffs, tell me, is it
    really me? Me against me?

Desert Scene

The night black as an eye and no light.

No water, life needs drained away.

Creatures with scales beneath and inside
and above, blooded beaked things.

Shell of the car rust-eaten, tires spinning
worlds. Car intact and hurtling, its people

braced captives, low sway of the radio gone
soft, a cowboy crooning to his dead girl.

The car speeding more from than to.

And the backseat kid fear like an awe
recognizable by its silence, squeezing out

the song and swallowing hard the desert
blanks, sand as if jamming the nose-throat,

and the mother's red hair too still, she grips
the wheel as an animal—

an animal run out, an animal run down—

and they'll spend the rest of their lives
getting over it.

Sex Worker

As I began
(however gently)
hair to influence:
with strange men
to engage in
two, just a
on the flight
begun climbing

inside me sat an adolescent trained
to use her brown eyes, breasts, soft
eventually, having strange sex
in exchange for cash, was just
an act for less than an hour or
terribly small move
of steps I'd already
down

Also inside me
a girl of a kind
life could grow
to her walls,
half-naked men,
a little girl who'd
for the dark
who'd never

a nun,
who still hoped, trusted
better, who nailed crosses
crosses strewn with little
men high up in death throes,
never taken off on a dirt bike
sparkle lights of LA, girl
taken off her top for anyone

Also inside me
and whore
cartoon extremes
life's big-top:
even a comfort,
members much
who get passed
and nothing

a clown, who found the nun
naive and abused, brutal outcomes,
like himself under
punchlines that felt familiar,
old jokes told by bigots or family
beloved, just words like women
over and down, over and around,
shifts

Daphne, Swimming

O, god of small children, what better than a pond?

Tree branches on the shore waving like a girl's arms, and there was little yet dividing us from ourselves.

Our needs were simple: somewhere to swim, someone to watch. A raft not too far out.

Beneath the muddy water, weeds that felt green. Most of us then unburned.

In the movies, a body of water portends drowning: we all had shadows without knowing and no one drowned—

or no one drowned in the pond, as a girl was swallowed whole by her uncle's hands.

What dried divine intervention?

If she could've swum from her body, she'd have turned into waves, gold-tipped, bound and unfrozen as a laurel tree on a summer shore.

Manifesto

One of the johns asks what my next job
will be. I understand that embedded in this
question is his real question, which is,
Will you continue my fantasy?
I think of my mother—one of the last things
she admitted to me was that when she was
five, she asked her mother for cowboy boots.
You mean cowgirl boots, her mother said.
No, cowboy boots, she said, having understood
even then it was better to move through this world

a man.

The john doesn't want a man. I know this, so
I say cowgirl, and he goes quiet, lying
back, his eyes glazed—and I start spinning
for him a picture of my naked body in leather
chaps, high-heeled boots. But in my head, I'm
spinning a rope above me like a noose, whipping
it down, tightening it hard about the neck
of a weaker being, so everyone watching will
see who does the riding, everyone watching
will know

who rules.

Hiker

It's December   it's cold   when I walk

city streets   by instinct   I duck my head

wrap my arms   around me   like fleece

though I shouldn't   be hiding   my body from

the elements   a sedan slows   the window glides

down it's cold   I duck my   head do not unfold

my arms but raise   my eyes looking   for warmth

in his smile   if I find it there   or not I hike

up my skirt to   close the deal   he unlocks

the door   remote   or pulls from his

inside coat   bills sometimes   a badge

an offering   what I can't know   is how the john

feels later   after we're   done

having gone   to an empty alley   where he undoes

and I bend   at the waist   perhaps he feels

betrayed   by his own   instinct his own

conscience   the women like me   who scare him

[...]

37

aroused	who remind him	his wife
mother	daughter could do	this
have done	this will	do

Clean

I take hot baths, one after each john, five or six
a day, though we're not supposed to waste water.
When Pimp Mike gets on my case, shoving a bill
in my face and adding on extra men, I switch to
whore's baths, filling the sink with water and lemon
soap, wetting the cloth. I wipe all over, then again
in the secret, moist places. I love you, sings the water,
I love you, sings the cloth, and I am very young,
almost embryonic, the water my father, the cloth
my mother, touching me pristine and in places
a tender feeling is not so strange.

Acknowledgments

I'm grateful to the sex workers I interviewed and whose stories I researched to inform this chapbook. All names and likenesses to actual individuals have been changed.

I'm grateful to the editors and readers who first accepted and published these poems (sometimes different versions or with different titles):

Cimarron Review: "Dilemmas" and "War"
Connotation Press (Best of 2017 Anthology): "Once in a Foreign City, I Saw a Dead Body"
Fourth River: "Mug Shot"
Hobart: "Runaways," "Sex Worker (Margaret Atwood)," and "Small Towns"
Jet Fuel Review: "Family," "Sex Worker (One year in The Life)"
Missouri Review: "Dirty Talk"
Moon City Review: "This Game Is a Rip"
Penn Review: "Clean"
Radar: "A Little TV"
Salt Hill: "Sex Worker (Out the apartment window)," "Smell of Pitch"
Southampton Review: "Daphne, Swimming," "Desert Scene"
South Dakota Review: "Crying for Money"
Tampa Review: "The Desperate Attract the Using"

My thanks and gratitude to the following:

Tim Green and the *Rattle* team for selecting *Backlit* and for an excellent collaborative experience.

My friends and family for their fellowship and support (editorial, emotional). I love you: Aimee, Airea, Andrew, Anne, Ben, Brennan, Britt, Brittany, Claudia, Dad, Deb, Dorsey, Erika, Jimmy, Judy H, Judy

M, Julie, Laura, Lisa, Lizzy, Lauren, Maria, Mason, Melissa, Mike, Mom, Patrick, Patty, Sara, Sif, Sus, Zack. In memory of Elaine.

And forever to Don. Ik hou van jou.

About the Rattle Chapbook Series

The Rattle Chapbook Series publishes and distributes a chapbook to all of *Rattle*'s print subscribers along with each quarterly issue of the magazine. Most selections are made through the annual Rattle Chapbook Prize competition (deadline: January 15th). For more information, and to order other chapbooks from the series, visit our website.

2025 | *no matter how it ends a bluebird's song* by Kat Lehmann
Haunt Me by José Enrique Medina
Backlit by Liz Robbins
2024 | *Cheap Motels of My Youth* by George Bilgere
In Which by Denise Duhamel
Sky Mall by Eric Kocher
2023 | *The Fight Journal* by John W. Evans
At the Car Wash by Arthur Russell
Plucked by Miracle Thornton
2022 | *Imago, Dei* by Elizabeth Johnston Ambrose
The Morning You Saw a Train of Stars … by CooXooEii Black
Visiting Her in Queens Is More Enlightening … by Michael Mark
2021 | *The Death of a Migrant Worker* by Gil Arzola
A Plumber's Guide to Light by Jesse Bertron
I Will Pass Even to Acheron by Amanda Newell
2020 | *Adjusting to the Lights* by Tom C. Hunley
A Juror Must Fold in on Herself by Kathleen McClung
Falling off the Empire State Building by Jimmy Pappas
2019 | *The Last Mastodon* by Christina Olson
Hansel and Gretel Get the Word on the Street by Al Ortolani
Did You Know? by Elizabeth S. Wolf
2018 | *To Those Who Were Our First Gods* by Nickole Brown
Tales From the House of Vasquez by Raquel Vasquez Gilliland
Punishment by Nancy Miller Gomez
A Bag of Hands by Mather Schneider
2017 | *In America* by Diana Goetsch
The Whetting Stone by Taylor Mali
2016 | *3arabi Song* by Zeina Hashem Beck
Kill the Dogs by Heather Bell
Ligatures by Denise Miller
Turn Left Before Morning by April Salzano

www.Rattle.com